Seeing Jesus Through the Eyes of A Grandma

Candice Bridges

ISBN (Paperback): 979-8-9884037-3-9
ISBN (eBook): 979-8-9884037-2-2

Dedication

Everett Ellington, my Dad, (for providing the money to publish.)

Pastor Wes Brown
(for giving me the opportunity to write a Bible Study)

Rev. Dr. Matt Mitchell
(for encouraging me to put the study into book form)

Gene Bridges (my husband)
(for his love, patience, and support)

Proofers: Ashley Smithey, Laura Mitchell, Doris Smith,
Diane Guy, Sunny Bolick, and Robbie Heilig

Encouragers: Brian Martindale and Libby Dalton

Grandchildren (Great-Grandchildren)
Chris/Holly (Connor, Jackson)
Shane/Rachel (Lukas, Emma Rae, Colby)
Hayden
Haley/Josiah (Ezra, Solomon)
Hannah
Katelyn (Noah)
Payton
Jacob
Levi

Table of Contents

Introduction to
Jesus Through the Eyes of
A Grandma

As we learned new words each week during our formative years in school, we became more and more interested in learning. We used what we already knew and built on that to learn more. We became hungry for knowledge, so we grew.

Each of us has a story of growth to share in our Christian walk. The story behind this book reads as follows: "My church was going to break into groups for our Wednesday night Bible Study, and my pastor, at that time, asked me to lead the lady's Bible study. After not agreeing on a book to study, I wrote one based on a basal reader that was full of family values. For 30 years this reader was used to teach children to read.

There is most likely not much new wisdom in these pages, but what I have gained over the years as a teacher, a parent, a grand and great-grand parent, a Christian, and a friend is presented here in a different way and hopefully will help you think about your life and how you are growing as a Christian.

What qualifies me to write? I have taught Kindergarten-College in my 36 years as a teacher. I have taught English as a second language in China through the English Language Institute of China.

I have been a Christian since childhood, wandered away from the Lord, and came back when my mother died in 1981. I have read the Bible through many times, studied many different Christian authors, listened to and internalized many sermons, and prayed extensively to gain a closer walk with the Lord. I hope you gain a closer walk with the Lord through this study.

CHAPTER 1

Words

Yes, I see the world differently. I am what is called an eternal optimist. I see things in books, circumstances, and people that others don't seem to see. I am a wife, mother, grandmother, and great-grandmother, and I learned to read using a basal reader. When I was young, my two older sisters taught my twin and I to read. They were learning and wanted us to share in their knowledge.

Those of you who are older remember learning to read from a basal reader that portrayed an almost perfect family consisting of a stay-at-home Mom, a working Dad, three children, a dog and a cat. You remember learning one word at a time, and that word repeated on each page with different illustrations to give the word more meaning. We were encouraged to look and see the things around us. Psalm 34:8 (ESV) (You Version Bible App. Crossway/ Goodnews Publishers 2001) (1) reads, "Oh taste and see that the Lord is good." Taste in Hebrew means "to perceive," and good means pleasant, so loosely translated here, we can say, "Perceive (look) and see that the Lord is pleasant." Let that sink in.

The message today is about words—how we use them—how they impact our life—how they impact others' lives. First, let's just list some words we know we use almost every day.

come	now	go	stay	pray
quiet	help	hello	good-bye	see you
love	please	hold it	dinner	thank-you

Make your own list of words and decide which words are encouraging and which are discouraging, which help, and which hurt.

Encouraging: Discouraging:

_______________________   _______________________

_______________________   _______________________

_______________________   _______________________

_______________________   _______________________

Most of us, at one time or another, have told our grandchildren that words can help us get our own way, express our thoughts, fill empty minutes, and sometimes they are our livelihood. Psalm 19:14 (ESV) (1) tells us, "Let the words of my mouth and the meditation of my heart be acceptable in Your sight, O Lord, my rock and my Redeemer."

With that in mind, consider this: Do you ever talk to yourself? Someone once said, "It is alright to talk to yourself, but when you start answering yourself, you are in trouble." What are some of the things you say to yourself that tend to make you feel good, bad, sad, or happy?

Good: Bad:

_______________   _______________

_______________   _______________

Can our words make a difference in how our day goes?

Reflect a moment on God's words found in Genesis 1:3,6,9, (ESV) (1). God said, "Let there be light, water, land, etc." Can our words be that powerful? How?

____

____

____

Think about a time when your words really encouraged someone. How did that make you feel? How did the person you encouraged feel? The other day I was talking to a friend and told her how much I appreciated the advice she had given me concerning a situation with my son. She was pleased that she had helped me, then, we were able to talk about many other things that we shared.

Look at Proverbs 1:1-7(ESV) (1). What did Solomon say about words?

They convey: 1   wisdom
                2   instruction
                3   understanding
                4   judgment
                5   justice
                6   knowledge

All these things come from the words we speak.

Who do you talk to the most?

____

____

How do your words make them feel?

____

____

How do their words make you feel?

____

____

What words do you speak each day that tell the Lord how you feel about Him?

____

____

____

____

There are so many ways we can use words to express or hide our true feelings.

Do your words sometimes make you laugh at yourself or make you smile? They need to! Words rule our lives, so we must choose them wisely. Now put into practice the use of words.

PRAYER: Lord, we pray our words will encourage and edify those we come into contact with each day. May our words be positive and up-lifting. Put a STOP sign in front of our faces each time we speak negatively.

CHAPTER 2

Up and Down

We remember bouncing our grandchildren on our knees while thinking about what they would become. We remember our own childhood and experiences that made us who we are today.

As we were introduced to each new character in our readers, we were introduced to new words and concepts. We learned to see interactions with the characters and their pets. We saw how the youngest child, Mary, played with her cat, Beau, in the swing. She liked to swing so much that she thought her cat would like to sit quietly in the swing and go back and forth and up and down repeatedly. The cat was not happy, so he jumped out and ran away.

There are three lessons that come to mind from this description.

1. God places us in His arms and says, "There will be ups and downs in your life, however, you can trust Me to keep you in them all.
2. As we live in Christ, we glide along and enjoy God at work in our lives.
3. We, as well, get impatient and "jump out of God's protective hands," thinking there is something better on the other side.

Going up and down also reminds me of birds. Birds are God's creation and He designed them to soar over the earth, depend on the earth for food and shelter, and land on the earth or in a tree to rest. The Lord also designed us for resting to be an important part of living.

Before continuing, we need to read the scripture upon which this chapter is based. Matthew 6:26. (ESV)(1) "Look at the birds of the air: they neither sow nor reap nor gather into barns, yet your Heavenly Father feeds them. Are you not of more value than they?"

"Worry has the connotation of dividing, separating, and distracting. People cannot worry and trust God at the same time, because worry destroys the single-hearted devotion Jesus describes in Matthew 6:33." (p. 1216 Women's Devotional Bible) (13).

When I am tempted to worry, I turn to the Psalms because they are songs that cause my heart to come in line with God's Word, and I can experience peace and rest with God. Pause now, and read Psalm 91, and make it personal. Change the personal pronouns to your name where appropriate.

He who dwells in the shelter of the Most High
Will abide in the shadow of the Almighty.
I will say to the Lord, "My refuge and my fortress,
my God, in whom I trust."
For He will deliver you from the snare of the fowler
    And from the deadly pestilence.
He will cover you with His pinions,
    and under His wings you will find refuge;
His faithfulness is a shield and buckler.
You will not fear the terror of the night,
    Nor the arrow that flies by day,
nor the pestilence that stalks in darkness,
nor the destruction that wastes at noonday.

A thousand may fall at your side,
    ten thousand at your right hand,
    but it will not come near you.
You will only look with your eyes
    and see the recompense of the wicked.
Because you have made the Lord your dwelling place
the Most High, who is my refuge—
no evil shall be allowed to befall you,
no plague come near your tent.
For He will command His angels concerning you
    to guard you in all your ways.
On their hands they will bear you up.
    Lest you strike your foot against a stone.

You will tread on the lion and the adder;
the young lion and serpent you will trample underfoot.
Because he holds fast to Me in love, I will deliver him;
I will protect him, because he knows My name.
When he calls to Me, I will answer him;
I will be with him in trouble;
I will rescue him and honor him.
With long life I will satisfy him and show him My salvation."

Did this exercise help you? In what ways?

____

____

____

____

What are some scriptures that you go to for help, peace and comfort?

______________   ______________   ______________

______________   ______________   ______________

Psalms are songs, written mostly by David, and we all know that he was a man after God's own heart. Over the years, I have come to believe that songs go straight to the heart. I believe this is scripturally based because of David's interaction with Saul in 1st Samuel 17:14-23. Reading Psalms brings peace to my soul.

I also use music to bring peace to me in troubled times. Three songs I link together to calm my spirit are: "I will come and bow down at your feet Lord Jesus,"(Ron Keenly, Zion Lyrics) (2) as I am "Sitting at your feet,(Brooklyn Tabernacle Choir) (3) while "I cast all my care upon You." (Kelly Faye Willard) (4)

I also use a chorus that I wrote and sing while worshipping.
"My eyes are lifted upward; my heart follows their gaze.
My soul is surrendered in adoration and praise.
My lips offer songs of love, my mind is stayed on You.
You are exalted, I am renewed.

My life is an open book, it's words speak of You
As daily I walk in all of Your truths.
Please keep me in places I can serve You best.
You are my peace, and in You I will rest."

Candy Bridges

Understand that I truly believe that just as God put songs in the bird's hearts, He places songs in our hearts to keep us gliding through the rough times in life. Psalm 8:6-9.

Are some days rougher than others? I believe they are.

When I was grieving my mother's death, my grandmother gave me a book called <u>Flight of the Wingless Bird</u> (Gibson Greeting Card Company, 1971)(5) which helped me greatly. It is no longer in print but I did Google it and found the whole book online. <u>Flight of the Wingless Bird.</u> Periwinkle Sue.com

Write about a time you felt God's presence in the midst of a stormy place in your life.

____

____

____

____

____

____

____

____

PRAYER: Lord, teach me how to worship You in all my Ups and Downs. Teach me how to help others worship You with abandon.

CHAPTER 3

Steadfastness

All of us at one time or another have wanted to be like a mountain—looked up to—steadfast—and beautiful. We feel this way because we trust the mountain not to crumble; but to remain where God placed it. Our trust in God is the same. He will never leave or forsake us. (Psalm 46:2) ESV (1)

Being a grandmother reminds me that trust in God and others is what helps us stay steadfast. From this basal, we remember that the father steadfastly comes home, so trust is built with his wife and his children. This issue of trust is carried out throughout this reader. We learned to trust our parents, grandparents, teachers, and others in authority through these lessons. Trust in God is like trusting that a mountain will not crumble or fall apart. Our trust is built over time just like the mountain. Sometimes our trust is shaken, but the mountain remains the same.

On the other hand, small rocks that fall from mountains are either shaken loose by the wind, rain, or even an earthquake. They might turn loose because the earth beneath them has eroded over time. Think for a minute about one sin you have committed during your lifetime. It may be just an impure thought, gossip, or even stealing candy from a store or your mom's cupboard. Did you start out to do something like that? No, but if you didn't recognize it as a sin and repent or ask forgiveness, the small thing allowed erosion to take place in your life.

Little things can come into our lives each day and become big issues when they are not "nipped in the bud." Think of any areas in your life that you have allowed to fester and cause unrest in your spirit until you sought forgiveness and turned from it. (List them below.) That is the way a mountain is built to become a fortress.

____

____

____

____

On a lighter note, as Christians, we see ourselves as "building our family" from the small things we do daily. What are some of the small things that we do to build character in our children and grandchildren? We teach them to clean up after themselves, right eating habits, to obey authority, how to dress appropriately, etc. These things build our family on a strong foundation.

Again, let's go back and think about the mountains God or we have placed in our lives. Everyone's mountain is not the same and none of us approach them in the same way. Some try to climb their mountain, some try to go around, and some try to go through. How are you dealing with your mountain? Are you searching for scripture? Praying? Talking with friends? Each of us sometimes stumbles and falls, but we get up again and start all over. We climb our mountain one step at a time.

Let me give you a personal experience to illustrate this point! One of the mountains I face daily is insecurity. I feel that I am not as pretty, outgoing, smart, lovable, successful in relationships, or as successful in other areas as others. Have I created my own mountain? Yes, and how do I climb that mountain? I seek out scripture that tells me that I am a child of God and that He created me to be who I am in Him. (Genesis 1:27, 1st Corinthians 6:19-20, 1st Peter 2:9) These are some of the scriptures I use when the discouraging thoughts come to me.

I encourage you to search for your own scriptures and write them out here.

____

____

____

____

Do you know how to find encouragement in the scripture? What are some of the ways you find scripture? I use a concordance or Google it.

Continuing with the way we handle our mountain; when we don't climb our mountain, we go around it. We find steps in the "rocks" that take us up a little higher. We don't realize we are climbing but we are with the Lord's help. It is through our steadfastness to not stay in the same place, plus God's steadfastness in moving us to move, that we are able to see our mountain for what it is, climb it, and be victorious. Be steadfast in your walk with God.

PRAYER: Lord, help us to trust You completely and unwaveringly. Teach us how to navigate our personal mountains, using Your Word as our guide. Keep Your loving arms around us as we face the mountains in our lives. Thank You.

CHAPTER 4

Life Happens

We have watched our grandchildren play and wondered if they would be injured by participating in a particular activity. We remember one story from the basal reader in which Mary is riding in her toy car, Mother is walking ahead, and Gene and Candy are following behind in the wagon. Everything seems to be fine, but we know something is going to happen. The car and the wagon are going faster and faster and Mary is heading for some baskets. Gene and Candy try to move over and end up tumbling over in the wagon.

There are many lessons to be learned from those few pages. What are some of the things you thought of?

____

____

____

____

____

Can we tell from the description whose fault it was? Does it really matter? No, but where do we go from here? Life Happens.

Let's look at something in nature that draws our attention to how life happens. A tree springs up from the ground leaving behind roots that grow deep into the soil. What happens to the tree if the roots don't grow deeply enough?

This lesson can be about establishing roots in our lives and how we help establish them in our family. First, let us think about how roots were established in our lives. Our parents, grandparents, neighbors, church, and schoolteachers helped establish our roots. What are some of the things that helped establish good roots? Some of them are prayer, Bible reading, obedience, and activities.

What does the Bible have to say about our roots? Proverbs 22:6 "Train up a child in the way he should go, even when he is old, he will not depart from it." (ESV) (1)

Some of us have children over who we claim this promise. Some of them are walking with the Lord and some are not. What went wrong? Free will! "You can lead a horse to water, but you can't make them drink." This is a humanistic saying, but it is true. We still trust the Lord and believe our child will turn around and come back to their roots, but we often blame ourselves for their behavior. We cannot do that because God gave each of us free will.

Let's look at this scripture in a different way, and it may help us. The scripture admonishes us to train our children in the way they should go. We have done that, now it is their responsibility to use that training in their lives. We can't do it for them.

Just as our children have roots, the tree has a base and branches that grow from the roots. It gets its nourishment from the roots and green leaves form and new life begins. So far, we have been focusing on the roots which are very important, but now, we need to turn our attention to the branches. Without the branches, the tree does not grow and spread.

As Christians, we are reminded through God's Word to "Go therefore and make disciples of all nations." Matthew 28:19 and Mark 16:15 "Go into all the world and proclaim the gospel to the whole creation." (ESV) (1). Does this mean that we must go to a foreign field to teach the gospel? Can we go into our homes, our workplace, our daily tasks teaching by the way we live?

Let us list some practical ways we can live out the gospel in our lives.

____

____

____

____

____

____

____

Yes, first, we must have His word hidden in our hearts so that we know how and what to share. We must search the Word when we have a problem so that we know what His Word says and tells us to do about the problem. (2nd Corinthians 1:3-4) (ESV) (1)

When we go and spread the good news, we must be so full of the knowledge of Christ that it spills out without us having to do anything. Name some Bible resources you can and do use to help you. The resources I use are Devotionals, Prayer Journals, and Bible apps.

____

____

____

____

____

____

To digress a little, look at the analogy of the tree. What happens to a tree when the roots get no or very little nourishment? Where do you see it first? Apply this to your life, examine yourself to see if your roots are getting enough nourishment. Ask God where you need to improve.

____

____

____

____

Fill in this chart with the number of hours you spend on each activity listed or create a chart of your own.

24 Hours

Sleeping _________________________   Cleaning/Working ________

Cooking and eating _________   Shopping ______________

Left over ____

What do you do with the "left over" hours? Make a list of what you do and about how much time you spend.

____

____

____

____

____

Now ask yourself if your roots are getting enough nourishment so you can branch out and help others to come to know Jesus. Are you allowing your life to just happen, or are you filtering it through God's eyes and Word? Use your list to help order your day to include time with God if that time is not already there. Determine where you can carve out some time or increase your time if needed.

In the first chapter you remember me telling you that I believe music goes straight to the heart. Because of this, an old hymn comes to mind here, and I will end this chapter with this:

PRAYER: May I   "Give of your(my) Best to the Master
Give of the strength of your(my) youth.
Throw your(my) souls fresh glowing ardor
Into the battle for truth."

Howard B. Gross
Baptist Hymnal (6)

CHAPTER 5

Beauty

Most of our grandchildren see us as beautiful. They see our love for them and we see the beauty the Lord has created in them.

BEAUTY! What is more beautiful than color? In our basal reader, we remember the excitement Mary portrayed when she learned her colors. Remember the awe you felt when you learned to read, many of you from this particular reader?

It is time to look at our Guide Book to determine what it says about colors and beauty. God shows us much more than a simple natural phenomenon when a rainbow appears in the sky after a rain. (Jacob Oelsen, Color Meanings) (11) Where is the rainbow mentioned in the Bible? Genesis 9:11-17 and Revelation 4:3. Take time to read each of those passages now.

Our focus today is Genesis 9:11-17. In verse 11, what did God tell Noah He was going to do?

What was the covenant?

____

____

____

____

We can cling to that promise no matter what floods come into our lives. God is there in the middle of them. He will "cover us with His feathers, and under His wings, we will trust." (Psalm 91:4) (ESV) (1)

What was the sign that God gave? Verses 12-13 tell us

____

____

Wow! A rainbow! What colors are in the rainbow, and what do they mean?

Red—Jesus' blood. passion, energy
Orange—Power, the presence of God
Yellow—gold
Green—vegetables, life
Blue—spirituality, heavens
Indigo—truth
Violet—royalty, priesthood

(I cannot find where I got this list, but it is not original to me.)

"We could spend much time here just thinking about the beauty God has given us to daily remind us of His care and love." <u>The Eagle Christian)</u> (Kenneth Price, Old Faithful Publishing Co./ Wetempka, Alabama, 1984; p. 7-9 (7)

In verses 14-17 of Genesis Chapter 9, God reminds us that He will remember His covenant. Read verse 16, "The rainbow shall be in the cloud, and I (God) will look on it to remember the everlasting covenant between God and every living creature of all flesh that is on the earth." (ESV) (1) That is us!

What else reminds us of the beauty of a relationship with God?

____

____

____

____

Ask my husband and he would say food. Food is nourishment, not just something that causes our bodies to become out of shape. Of course, we all know the scripture that tells us that "our bodies are the temple of God, we are not our own, we were bought with a price." (1st Corinthians 6:19) (ESV) (1) That was for free, we need to pull our focus back to nourishment. What nourishes our bodies?

____

____

____

What nourishes our souls?

____

____

____

It is strange that the food pyramid is something we have followed all our lives, but it has changed many times, however, the Word never changes.

The base of the pyramid used to be bread, cereal, rice, and pasta. Now, what do most diets tell us about bread, cereal, and pasta?

____

____

____

What is the world trying to tell us about the Bread of Life?

____

____

____

We must build our lives on the Bread of Life. What is added on the next level? Faith. We associate Jesus with faith because faith is "the assurance of things hoped for, the conviction of things not seen." (Hebrews 11:6) (ESV) (1)

What does the Bible tell us about nourishing or building on our faith? (2nd Peter 1:5-7) ESV (1)

____

____

____

____

These verses tell us to nourish our faith by building upon it virtue. "Virtue" is showing high moral standard. We add to that knowledge and self-control. For many, this is where our nourishment pyramid begins to crumble, especially where food is concerned. How about spiritually? Is self-control a problem for you? Only you can answer that, so be honest with yourself.

Pray about it, ponder it, and do a self-check.

____

____

____

____

____

To self-control, we are to add perseverance—sticking to what we are doing until we get it right. Then we add Godliness, brotherly kindness, and love.

How did we get from colors and beauty to this examination? Our lives should be beautiful for God!

I believe the Holy Spirit is prompting me to go back to self-control and examine that more closely so we can proceed with a solid foundation. Self-control implies so many different things in so many areas of our lives. Name some things we need to exercise self-control over in order to be good Christians? How do we control ourselves?

____

____

____

____

When we control our thoughts, we can soar above the everyday problems that try to overtake us. What are your first thoughts each morning?

____

____

____

In Kenneth Price's book <u>The Eagle Christian</u>, (7) he states: "It has been said humorously, 'you are what you eat'." This is true spiritually also. What parts of the Bible do you devour daily? What are some of your favorite scriptures and why are they your favorite?

____

____

____

____

Think about some of the scriptures you have committed to memory. Do you still commit scripture to memory? I honestly believe it is dangerous these days not to have scripture memorized, even if you don't know the "address," you know the scripture. In the past, I used a concordance each time I needed to find where a scripture was in the Bible, but now there is Google.

Tips for memorizing scripture can be found in many places, in fact there is an App, *Verses*, that will help you. We must remember Hebrews 4:12 and Psalm 119:11 to help us realize the necessity of having God's Word in our hearts. We will be a more beautiful Christian when we do that.

PRAYER: Our Father, who art in Heaven, hallowed be Thy Name. Thy Kingdom come, Thy will be done, on earth as it is in heaven. Give us this day our daily bread and forgive us our debts as we forgive our debtors. Lead us not into temptation but deliver us from evil. For Thine is the kingdom, the power, and the glory forever! Amen (ESV) (1) Matthew 6:5-15.

CHAPTER 6

Sharing

Grandmothers are always teaching their grands about sharing. They encourage them to share with each other, their friends, and their family.

In this basal reader, we learned sharing on almost every page. The whole family was always sharing family time, and the children shared with each other. We recall the example of how Mary unwittingly shared her ice cream with her pets. Mother and the children are purchasing ice cream. Bubba and Beau are outside the store looking in. When the family exits the shop, both pets jump on Mary and her ice cream ends up on the sidewalk. Bubba and Beau lick it up.

What are some of the things we share purposefully or not?

What does the Bible say about sharing? Matthew 28:18-20 and Mark 16:15 tell us to go into all the world and preach the gospel to everyone. It has been said that "there are two things the believer and non-believer have in common: they are both are uptight about evangelism." (Greg Laurie) (<u>Tell Someone</u> Harvest Ministries 2003; Online Course) (8)

I have asked myself many times why I am so unsure or awkward about sharing the gospel of Christ. Our pastor has often told us that we will share that about which we are most passionate. I remember when I first gave my heart and life back to Jesus, I would recite Psalm 23 in this way, and share it enthusiastically with anyone who would listen.

"The Lord is Candy's shepherd,
She shall not want.

Now turn in your Bibles and read Psalm 23 with me, inserting your name where there is an "I" or "my".

He makes ___________ to lie down in green pastures
He leads ____________ beside still waters.
He restores __________'s soul.
He leads ____________ in the paths of righteousness for His name's sake.
Even though ___________ walks through the valley of death, ____________ will fear no evil.
For God is with _________________,
His rod and His staff will comfort ________________.
God prepares a table before ___________ in the presence of __________'s enemies.
God anoints ________________'s head with oil.
________________ cup overflows.
Surely goodness and mercy will follow ________________

all the days of _________________'s life,
And _________________ will dwell in the house of the Lord
forever." (ESV) (1)

When read this way, doesn't it give us a sense of joy in the Lord? Doesn't is give us an empowerment to want to go and teach the gospel?

One practice Gene, my husband, and I have when we go out to eat is to ask our waiter or waitress what we can pray about for them as we ask our blessing. The responses we receive would be a book by itself. Most times we have positive feedback. It was awkward at first, but now it is second nature unless the Holy Spirit prompts us not to ask.

Write some other scriptures that fill us with joy.

____

____

____

____

Examples: Isaiah 1:18; 6:1-5; Psalm 42:1-2(ESV) (1)

When we read the scriptures aloud, and as personal messages from God, they give us a renewed sense of just how much God loves us and wants us to share Him with others.

"Come now, Let us reason together" (With whom are we reasoning?) We are one with the Lord. "Though your sins be as scarlet, they shall be as white as snow." Hallelujah! Let that sink in. "Though they are red like crimson, they shall be as wool." (ESV) (1) (Imagine the worst thing you have ever done being washed away by the blood of Jesus.)

Isaiah 6:1-3: "In the year King Uziah died, I saw the Lord!" (ESV) (1)

Wow! When was the last time you saw the Lord?

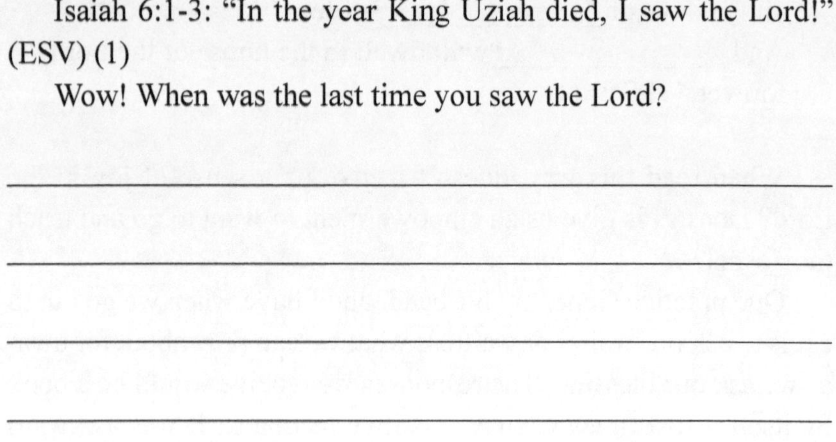

"He was high and lifted up, and His train filled the temple. (When we praise and lift Him up, His Presence fills us and the place we are worshipping.) "So we cry, Holy, Holy, Holy, is the Lord of Hosts; the whole earth is full of His glory." (ESV) (1). These words make me fall in love with Jesus all over again. They fill my spirit with awe!

Turn to Psalm 42:1 "as the deer pants for the water, so my soul pants for You, O God. My soul thirsts for God, for the living God....." (ESV) (1)

After we fill ourselves with the reminder of who God is in us, what He has done for us, and who we are in Him, we are ready to fulfill the great commission, "Go Ye into all the world." (Mark 16:15-16.) (ESV) (1)

Greg Laurie in his book <u>Tell Someone</u>, (9) tells us that "We all have a sphere of influence; people we work with, people we live beside, people we engage with daily: Family, the Workplace, our Neighborhood, the World, are some examples."

I still cringe sometimes when I try to share, but then I remember Esther: "For if you keep silent at this time, relief and deliverance will arise for the Jews from another place, but you and your father's house will die. And who knows whether you have not come to the kingdom for such a time as this?" (Esther 4:14) (ESV) (1)

"We must remember that everyone's favorite subject is themselves. Encourage them, ask a person about their life, their views, their outlook. Then lovingly begin to build your bridge to them. Remember we are just beggars telling another beggar where to find food." Greg Laurie. (8)

I know by now some of you are thinking, "I just can't do something like that, or I don't have the opportunity." Here, I refer you to Shirley Duncan. Shirley is always sharing on Facebook about how the Lord uses her daily in others' lives. A friend of mine, Libby Dalton is another person who looks for ways to serve the Lord daily. She has written a book Libby's Christmas Letters, (Libby's Christmas Letters Libby Dalton, Genesis Publishing 2023) (9) in which she relates many stories of how God has used her in everyday life.

Rest assured that when you fill yourself, it will spill out. Take some time now to write out your own testimony.

____

____

____

____

____

____

____

PRAYER: Lord, may my testimony be an encouragement for a fellow believer, an enticement for someone to come to know you, or both.

CHAPTER 7

Work

We grandmothers have worked all our lives to make a difference in the lives of our spouses, our children, and many times our grandchildren. We desired to instill a great work ethic into their lives and those in our sphere of influence.

In this part of our study, we will focus on work. From the beginning of the book, we see Dad going off to work and Mom staying at home with the children. This is truly not the norm in our world today. Some men stay home while the woman works. What is your view of this practice?

____

____

____

____

____

Did you or do you work while your children go to school or day care?

____

____

____

Did or do you teach your children to work?

____

____

____

____

What did we learn from our basal reader about work? Recall the story in which Gene is painting chairs, and Mary is cleaning her room. The funny thing is that Mary puts everything under her bed instead of putting them where they belong.

The lesson that jumped out to me is how sometimes we sweep things "under the rug," or "hide them in the closet," thinking no one will see. Some of the things I tend to sweep under the rug or hide in the closet are decisions I need to make that will alter what I need to do each day. Some examples are writing that card, sending that text, visiting that friend, or keeping that promise to pray diligently for a request that has come to me. I do feel I have gotten better about this with God's help and reminders.

1st Thessalonians 4:9-11 (ESV) (1) reads: "Now, about your love for one another, we do not need to write to you, for you yourselves have been taught by God to love each other. And, in fact, you do love all of God's family throughout Macedonia. Yet we urge you, brothers and sisters, to do so more and more, and to make it your ambition to lead a quiet life: You should mind your own business and work with your hands, just as we told you, so that your daily life may win the respect of outsiders and so that you will not be dependent on anybody."

How did we learn our work ethic?

____

____

____

____

____

Is everyone's work ethic the same?

____

____

____

____

____

How does our work ethic affect others?

____

____

____

____

Does our work ethic ever change?

____

____

____

____

How do we work daily for the Lord?

____

____

____

____

To what extent can we carry the Lord into our workplace?

____

____

____

____

____

Some of us work in our homes, so we must discipline ourselves to get everything accomplished each day. Is working at home of any less value than the work we do in the marketplace?

____

____

____

____

What are some of the advantages of working from home?

____

____

____

____

What are some of the disadvantages?

____

____

____

All avenues of work are valid and important. Even though some of us are retired, we still have the responsibility of keeping things running smoothly in our homes.

You may give the "church" answer to this question. What Is one of the most important things we can do for ourselves each day that will improve our life?

____

____

____

____

With such busy schedules, how do we accomplish this?

____

____

____

____

To close, let's review some scriptures that help us remember what God says about working. Even if you are not working in the marketplace, you are working every day to live the best Christian life you can. (Biblereasons.com) (11)

Leviticus 9:11	Colossians 1:10	Proverbs 22:1
Proverbs 20:23	Deuteronomy 15:13-14	Romans 12:2
Psalm 128:2		
Colossians 3:23	Proverbs 28:6	Proverbs 19:17
Isaiah 1:17a	Colossians 3:17	Matthew 6:24

Read each of these scriptures and maybe add some of your own to determine which ones will help you personally. Write out how they can help you.

____

____

____

____

____

____

One of the best Christian work habits we can establish and maintain is that of praying for others. Pray each time God brings a person to your mind.

What have you learned thus far from your memories of the stories from which you learned to read.?

____

____

____

____

PRAYER: Lord, may we help others in the teaching of work ethic by the way we live.

CHAPTER 8

Relationships

We fondly look back to the lives our children led. We also look daily at the lives our grandchildren are leading. We have a bond with our grandchildren that no one else can have.

We recall from our readers that this family has good, bonding relationships. They spend a lot of time together. Families grow when they spend quality time together.

Some characteristics of good relationships are trust, confidence, love, helpfulness, praise, communication, honesty, dependability, and commitment.

This family exhibits these characteristics continuously.

I believe that this is where I need to insert a poem I once wrote about relationships. (<u>Celebrate Poets Speak Out</u>, Spring 2003. Creative Communications, Inc. p. 148)(11)

How Does Your Marriage Garden Grow?

How does your marriage garden grow?
    Are all your flowers in a row?
Do you plant more flowers than you can pick?
    By giving more compliments than you seek.

Do you water regularly, verbally, and sincere?
Do affirmation of strength and abilities they hear?

Is your garden getting enough SON exposure?
Through encouragement and development of learning
together?
What about food? Does it get enough?
Are there gifts, fruits, treats, dates, and all such stuff?
Is there enough "hands on" attention to the flowers?
    Hugs, kisses, handholding, talking for hours?

Are you pulling the weeds that daily creep in?
    Ugly words, unforgiveness, anger, and sin?
Are you gently removing the weeds and thorns?
    So that horrible scars won't be born?

Do you seek the Master Gardner in prayer?
    Together and separately, giving great care.
So your marriage garden will grow just right!
    And your happiness will last night after night.

Candy Bridges

Marriage is one of the greatest relationships in our lives, along with that of a relationship with God. Name some other healthy relationships in your life.

46

According to the Bible, the first relationship was the Trinity, then God and Adam, then Adam and Eve. Man, and Satan, ruined the relationship with Adam, Eve, and God. However, there are some other true relationships in the Bible as seen in David and Jonathan. (1st Samuel (18:1-3). There is advice about close friends in Proverbs 18:24. We can name many more relationships and friendships, but who is the friend that sticks closer than a brother?

____

____

____

____

We must be careful in choosing any of our relationships, and also what we do to keep them. Name some things you would be willing to do for a friend or a family member.

____

____

____

____

Let's have a little fun. Think about a time you spent with your grandchildren. Remember the first time you held them in your arms? Remember the love that flowed from you to them? Remember the instant bonding? Remember how you just wanted to be their mentor and friend?

Does anyone understand where I am going with this? Is Jesus your friend?

____

____

____

____

How do you know?

____

____

____

____

Do you spend quality time with Him each day?

____

____

____

Do you laugh with Him?

____

____

____

____

Think about a time when you laughed with Jesus.

____

____

____

____

Do you cry with Jesus?

____

____

____

____

Ask yourself some serious questions. Do I spend daily time with Him? Do I long for His Presence to be with me? Can I invite Him with me wherever I go? Can I invite him to watch TV or listen to the music I listen to? Do you and your friends spend time with Him?

If you are like me, there are areas in which I can improve. I am reminded of the book, <u>The Eagle Christian (7)</u>. It encourages us to compare our lives to the eagle. Can we aspire, like the eagle, to "fly at altitudes where no other bird flies, and observe the earth from afar? He does not want to be with other birds who do not wish to fly higher. The eagle has experienced what most birds will never know." (The Eagle Christian) (7)

Because I cannot say it any better, I will quote directly from Kenneth Price. "Is this not a picture of the Eagle Christian who will not submit himself to the nature of others who spend all of their time in activities of one sort or another and never learn the ways of the high winds of the spirit. To really walk with God, the Eagle Christian must pursue solitude, not as an escape, but rather to be alone with God and learn the ways of the Spirit of God." "Leaving those things which lie behind" we press ever forward. Philippians 3:13-14 Isaiah 40:31 (The Eagle Christian p. 48) (7)

PRAYER: May we strive to strengthen our relationship with the Lord every day and may His presence manifest Himself in our daily lives.

CHAPTER 9

Family

We smile when we think about family. We look at pictures of times with family and reminisce. Relationships are seen best through the institute of family. If you are doing this study by yourself, or in a group, spend some time viewing pictures of your family. Tell who is in each picture, whether they are still living or living with you. Talk or think about your family and what they mean to you. From our memories of the basal reader, we see the whole family together.

The family is going on vacation, or so it seems. Everyone is helping prepare and the pets sense something is happening. Beau hides in the car, but Bubba is told that he cannot go. The family gets into the car and is surprised to see Beau on the floorboard. Gene looks out the window of the moving car and discovers Bubba on the running board. The whole family is indeed going on the trip.

This leads us to wonder what the Bible has to say about family. God establishes the family in Genesis 1:28. "And God blessed them and God said to them, 'be fruitful and multiply and fill the earth and subdue it, and have dominion over the fish of the sea and over the birds of the heavens and over every living thing that moves on the earth'." (ESV) (1)

There are several scriptures that give us advice about how to live in a family atmosphere. We will explore one scripture for each family member. Proverbs 31:15. 1st Timothy 3:4-5, 1st Timothy 5:8, and Ephesians 6:1 are some we will use.

Proverbs 31 is a well-known Proverb that gives advice to wives and mothers. "She rises while it is yet night and provides food for her household and portions for her maidens." (Proverbs 31:15) (ESV) (1)

What are your thoughts about this scripture?

____

____

____

____

Do you ever feel overwhelmed by this? Why or why not?

____

____

____

____

Never fear, the Bible also gives advice to the father of the family. In 1st Timothy 3:4-5, the Deacon of the church is told, "He must manage his own household well, with all dignity, keeping his children submissive." (ESV) You say, "that advice is for deacons in the church," but how much better it would be for families if the Father were indeed the head of the house. We are also reminded in 1st Timothy 5:8 "But if anyone does not provide for his relatives and especially for members of his household, he is denied the faith and is worse than an unbeliever." (ESV) (1)

The children are not left out. Ephesians 6:1(ESV) (1)"Children, obey your parents in the Lord, for this is right." Do you remember how, throughout the basal reader the children are obedient to their parents? They were even obedient to each other. This book does portray an ideal family, I know. It sets a standard which we should strive to achieve. Imagine your perfect family.

____

____

____

____

Are there some changes you need to make in order to achieve a perfect family?

____

____

____

____

Does that mean we have it all wrong? No, if our family values are based on God's Word, we have it all right, even if it does not seem that way.

Prayerfully consider what you are doing right.

____

____

____

____

Even though we all do not have as perfect a family as we wish, we can strive to do this by basing our family values on God's Word.

Concentrate on that and listen for God to lead you in what changes need to be made. Remember, "You eat an elephant one bite at a time." (Desmond Tutu). Considered to be an African Proverb.

PRAYER: Lord, as parents and grandparents, help us guide our children in Your will and way.

CHAPTER 10

Comparisons

Do we, as grandmothers, compare our grandchildren to their parents or our great grands to their parents?

"Big and Little" is the title of one of the chapters in the reader we are referencing. In these pages, the parents are measuring the physical growth of their children. They are discussing who is big and who is little. Mary seems a little discouraged until she realizes her bear, Meshi is shorter than she.

Even as Christians, we are prone to compare ourselves to others. In a previous chapter, I mentioned that I was and sometimes still am very insecure. That insecurity not only stems from my life experiences (rejection, divorce, failure), but also from my tendency to compare myself to others.

Can some comparisons be helpful? How?

Can some be harmful? Why?

____

____

____

Theodore Roosevelt once said, "Comparison is the thief of joy", but what does God say? Let us search the scriptures to determine what God says about comparing ourselves to others. I used Biblereasons.com (11) to find these references,

Galatians 6:45

____

____

____

2nd Corinthians 10:12

____

____

____

Your thoughts?

____

____

____

____

____

____

____

1st Thessalonians 4:11-12 (ESV (1) tells us, "But we urge you, brothers, to do this more, and mind your own affairs, and to work with your hands, as we instructed you. That you may walk properly before outsiders, and be dependent on no one."

I specifically chose to write this scripture because it has helped me in my marriage more than once. I asked the Lord to keep my mouth shut, especially in the early years of our marriage, to keep arguments to a minimum. It has worked, and even though this is a second marriage for both of us, we celebrated 26 years in April 2023. Comparisons in a second marriage are harmful when you are comparing spouses and problems. With the Lord's help, we have been able to avoid these types of comparisons.

The greatest thing to remember about comparisons is who we are to use as our greatest comparison. Our highest achievement is living for Jesus. We will not achieve perfection as Jesus is perfect until we reach eternity. However, we can strive to emulate Jesus' character and compare our thoughts and actions to that.

Jesus	**Me**
Honest	_______________
Truthful	_______________
Compassionate	_______________
True	_______________
Loving	_______________

This is just a little exercise to show us how much we can improve and strive for perfection.

We can use comparison to tear ourselves down or build ourselves up. In the beginning of this chapter, I asked you to list some harmful comparisons. Can you change those into helpful?

____

____

____

____

____

____

____

Let us end this study about comparisons thinking positively about who we are in Christ (From OnlyJesusMinistry.com)(12)

New creation (2ⁿᵈ Corinthians 5:7)   Complete in Him (Ephesians 2:5)

God's Masterpiece (Ephesians 2:10   Child of God (1ˢᵗ John 3:1)

Dearly Loved (Colossians 3:12)   Blessed (Galatians 3:9)

Holy Spirit's Temple 1ˢᵗ Cor. 6:19)   Chosen (1ˢᵗ Thess.1:4)

Being changed into His image (2ⁿᵈ Corinthians 3:18)

As you meditate on who you are in Christ, choose one or two of these scriptures to make personal:

"I am…____

____

____

____

____

Comparing ourselves in this way is such an encouragement to continue growing in Christ.

PRAYER: "Lord prepare me to be a sanctuary, pure and holy, tried and true. With thanksgiving, I'll be a living, sanctuary for You. (Maranatha Music) written by Randy Lyn Scruggs, John W. Thompson. Album/ Top 100 Praise and Worship Songs 2nd Edition. Released 2012. (13)

CHAPTER 11

Wants and Desires verses Need

We recall that at one time during our reading, the mother and her three children are in a bakery and seeing many things they want. They purchase something from the counter to satisfy their wants. These bakery items are wants or desires, not needs. Did the "want" cause them to "desire", or the "desire" cause them to "want"?

This is the way in our Christian walk. When we desire a closer walk with God, we want to absorb all we can of Him. There are many scriptures that point us to the differences between wants or desires and needs. The one that pops to mind first is found in James 4:3 (ESV) (1) "You ask and do not receive, because you ask wrongly, to spend it on your passion."

Do you know the difference between your wants/desires and needs.

WANTS/DESIRES	**NEEDS**
Long-Arm Quilter	To be financially secure
____	___________________________________
____	___________________________________
____	___________________________________
____	___________________________________

When we truly examine our wants, we can determine if they will benefit us in the long run. We must also ask ourselves the question, "Will it draw me closer to the Lord or distract me?" Through lots of prayer, we can answer that question. Is it sometimes disappointing when you realize your want or desire is not something God has in mind for you?

An example from my personal life resulted in the writing of this book. I want to keep my mind sharp as I grow older, so I began to play word games, and to be honest, thinking games on my iPad each day. This resulted in my spending an hour or more each day on the games. I knew I was "wasting daylight" but could not make myself quit. I found myself apologizing to the Lord for spending more time on games than with Him.

For Lent this year, I asked the Lord what He wanted for me in the area of fasting. He impressed upon me it was the time I was spending on the games. I then asked Him how I was to keep my mind sharp, and He "told" me to write that book I had wanted to write for many years. I prayed long and hard and began a search for the cost. The Lord, "opened the door that needed to be opened."

(A paraphrase of Revelation 3:7). He does let us know the difference in our wants and needs and provides ways to access our needs as well.

The value we ascertain here is: Does my want turn into an obsession? How we react to the want is our decision. Find some scripture that helps you distinguish between the two.

Matthew 6:25-34   Luke 15:12-17
_______________________   _______________________

_______________________   _______________________

_______________________   _______________________

Another example is the one I referred to in the chart on p. 62. I am a Quilter and have learned how to free motion quilt. Even though I have a stitch regulator, my stitches are often uneven. My quilting area is small, but that is about to change. I often have a hard time rolling the quilt under the throat of my machine. A long arm quilter would solve both the problem of the stitches and the crowding under the throat of my machine. My husband is building a sewing room for me, so I thought this would be a perfect opportunity to purchase a long-arm quilting machine. After much prayer and research on cost verses usage, I decided the expense was not worth it. After all, I am 77 and how many more years do I have to quilt? That does not get rid of the desire, it just puts it into perspective.

Is there any area in your life where your wants and needs clash?

____

____

____

If only life could be as simple as it was in the book from which we learned to read. I want sweets, I purchase sweets and consume them, no thought to the weight gain, LOL! That is a whole new area of wants/desires verses needs. Too many books have been written on that topic, so I will leave it alone. I do believe though that I need to discuss my weight with God, listen to what He says, and obey even if I don't want to. Reflect, if you will, on those thoughts.

PRAYER: Lord, give me insight and wisdom in my daily activities so I can discern readily between wants and needs.

CHAPTER 12

Persistence

If you have made it this far in the study, you have been persistent and resisted the temptation to quit in "mid-stream." You most likely have examined your walk with God and discovered areas in which you can improve. I know I did while writing.

Examining our memories one last time, we see the persistence of Mary and the construction workers to restore Meshi into her possession. She had accidentally dropped Meshi into the pit where the workers were digging. She asks her dad or brother to jump down and get him. They cannot, but the construction worker brings him up with a load of dirt. Meshi is restored into Mary's arms.

There are so many lessons in this story, but the one that stands out the most comes from Isaiah 40:31, "But they that wait for the Lord shall renew their strength; they shall mount up with wings like eagles; they shall run and not be weary; they shall walk and not faint." (ESV) (1)

How hard is it to be persistent but wait for the Lord in the meantime? That sometimes seems like an impossible task, but other scriptures teach us to persist as we are waiting. Biblereasons. com (11) gives us these:

Matthew 15:2

James 1:4

1st Corinthians 16:11

Psalm 107:19

____

____

____

____

____

Choose one of these, or one of your own and describe what it means to you. Mary's pleas and the construction workers' persistence paid off with good results. Look closely at the meaning here. We need to persist in our daily living to "settle inside" with Jesus and not be on the outside looking in. Write some of the insights you have gained from this study. Which chapter "hit you the hardest?" "Why?" How have you changed?

____

____

____

____

____

PRAYER: Lord, may we continue growing closer to you as we continue to study Your Word

Acknowledgements

1. ESV You Version App. Crossway/Goodnews Publishers 2001

2. Ron Keenly Zion Lyrics (I Will Come and Bow Down at Your Feet, Lord Jesus)

3. Brooklyn Tabernacle Choir (Sitting At His Feet)

4. Kelly Faye Willard (I Cast All My Care Upon You)

5. Gibson Greeting Card Company 1971. (Flight of the Wingless Bird)

6. Howard B. Gross Baptist Hymnal Convention Press. Nashville Tennessee 1956. P. 353 (Give of Your Best to the Master)

7. The Eagle Christian Kenneth Price. Old Faithful Publishing Co./Wetempka, Alabama 1984.

8. Greg Laurie Tell Someone Harvest Ministries 2003

9. Libby Dalton, Libby's Christmas Letters. Genesis Publishing Company, 2023.

10. <u>Celebrate. Poets Speak Out</u> . Spring 2003 Creative Communications Inc. p. 148.

11. Web Resources: Bible Reasons.com.; OnlyJesusMinistry.com; Jacob Olesen Color Meanings.com

12. Maranantha Music written by Randy Lynn Scruggs, John W. Thompson, Album/Top 100 Praise and Worship Songs 2nd Edition. Released 2012.

13. Women's Devotional Bible copywrite 1995, Thomas Nelson Inc. NKJV. Used by permission. All rights reserved.